Contents

Cutting open   4

Ancient times   6

The Middle Ages   12

Blood, boils and burns   18

Ground-breaking   24

In the wars   34

Modern times   40

Find out more   52

Glossary   53

Index   56

Any words appearing in the text in bold,
like this, are explained in the glossary.
You can also look out for them in the Word
bank at the bottom of each page.

Cutting open

A scalpel is a surgeon's small steel knife. It makes clean and narrow cuts into skin and flesh. Thousands of years ago scalpels were made of flint or bone. Their job was just the same as it is today – cutting open bodies.

If a car breaks down, it may need a new part. That could mean a quick fix or a major repair job. Either way, it will need special tools and a careful look under the bonnet. It is just the same when a body goes wrong! A **surgeon** may need to look inside. Parts may need to be patched up or taken away.

Surgery makes us think of sharp blades, blood, needles, sore wounds and scars. But surgery today is very different from years ago. The surgeon's **scalpel** once meant bad news.

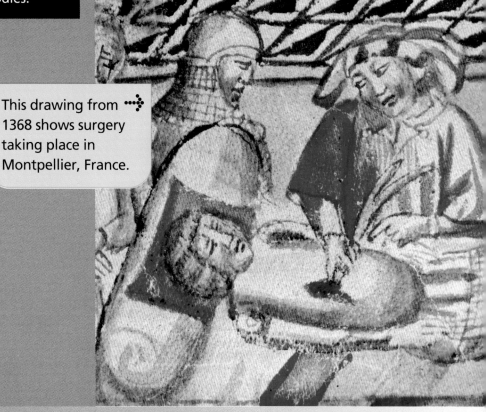

This drawing from 1368 shows surgery taking place in Montpellier, France.

4

Word bank

surgeon doctor who operates on the body and treats injuries

Blood and guts

Surgery used to be very risky. There was a lot of blood, guts, stitches, scabs and scars. If you needed an operation, you had to lie wide-awake on a table. You screamed in agony as the blade cut into you. Strong men held you down.

Surgeons never washed their hands before they cut into your body. They had to stitch your muscles and skin back together quickly to stop you bleeding to death. It was touch and go whether you would **survive**.

Find out later...

Why did surgeons have to cut off legs so fast?

Why did barbers try to make their customers bleed?

Why don't surgeons always need their scalpels today?

survive   stay alive despite danger and difficulties

Skulls

Ancient skulls with holes cut through them have been dug up around the world. They have been found in Europe, Asia and South America. Sometimes the bone that was cut out was worn on string around the patient's neck after the operation.

Thousands of years ago, treating pain involved a lot of guesswork. People sometimes learned how to do very basic surgery. It was by having a go that they found out what worked best. It is only because of all this blood and pain that **surgeons** today have become so skilful.

Today a bad headache is usually cured with drugs. Thousands of years ago things were very different. The doctor might have knocked a hole in your head with a chisel to try to let out the pain!

Drilling a hole through a patient's skull in 1880.

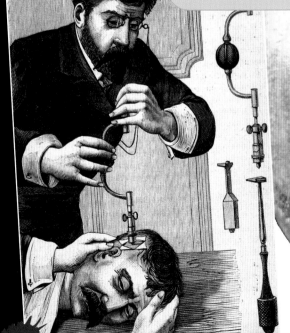

Word bank

pressure force that builds up in a space and cannot escape

Holes in the head

Skulls of people who died 10,000 years ago have been found with holes drilled in them. Some skulls have up to 5 holes. Some holes are 5 centimetres wide. They may have been drilled to let out "evil spirits" or to cure bad headaches. The bone often began to grow back around the holes, showing that some patients **survived**. The name for this operation is **trepanning**.

A trepanned skull from over 1000 years ago.

Easing the pressure

Easing the pressure

In 1998 Hayden McGlinn was playing football in Australia when he hit his head and collapsed. A doctor called Hindley was close by. He thought Hayden was bleeding inside his brain. He quickly drilled a hole into Hayden's head to let out the pressure. It did the trick and he survived.

Fast facts

Trepanning was still done 150 years ago to help people with mental illness. This was thought to release **pressure** inside the head.

Making use of nature

People long ago had to use anything they could find for surgery. For **scalpels** they used sharp bones, sticks and stones. To stitch the skin back together, some people even used ants!

South American Indians living in the rainforests gathered army ants. These ants are only about 2 centimetres long but they have big pincer-like jaws. The ants were held over two flaps of skin with their jaws open. When they bit, their jaws clamped the wound shut. When the ant's body was pinched off, its head was left behind like a stitch in the skin, holding the wound together.

Tools of the trade

Over 2500 years ago medicine in India included surgery. An Indian **surgeon's** sharp tools were knives, scissors, saws and needles. Blunt tools such as **forceps**, levers, hooks and probes were made from the materials found in the forests.

Some of the tools that were used for surgery in Algeria, Africa.

Word bank **Aborigine**   native Australian person

Bones

If you break your arm, it is usually easy for doctors to fix it. When the arm is set in solid plaster, the broken bone is held still so it can mend.

But how did people cope with broken arms long ago? Ancient people like the **Aborigines** of Australia knew just what to do. They dug wet clay out of the ground. Then they wrapped it around the broken arm and let it dry in the sun. It soon set solid – just like a modern plaster cast.

Healing

The ancient Egyptians did simple surgery. Some of their bronze tools have been found in the pyramids. They put tree bark on surgical wounds to stop them getting infected.

The strong jaws of an army ant. This photo has been enlarged many times.

Fast facts

Australian Aborigines put clay or animal fat over cuts. This would help the scars to heal.

forceps   surgical pincers used to hold and grasp things

Roman and Greek surgeons

Over 2000 years ago, the Romans and the Greeks learned a lot about surgery. Roman **surgeons** used knives and saws to cut off soldiers' infected arms and legs. They also knew how to stitch wounds to stop bleeding.

One operation was named after the Roman ruler Julius Caesar. His mother had problems giving birth to him so he was cut out of her **womb**.

This is now called a **Caesarean** birth. It is often used today if the mother or baby is in difficulty. But 2000 years ago, it was very risky and was only done if the mother died and the baby was still alive inside her.

Stitch-up

For centuries, surgeons have used stitches to close up wounds. They can be used inside the body or for holding skin together so it can heal. People long ago used thread made of fine leather, horsehair, wool, silk or cotton.

Stitching up a wound in the head today can be almost painless.

Word bank

abdomen   area of the body below the chest, containing
the stomach

Galen

Galen was a Greek doctor, born in AD 129. He became a surgeon to the Roman **gladiators** so he had to stitch many nasty wounds.

Galen was one of the first surgeons to use **catgut** for stitches. He became well known for saving many gladiators' lives. Some had stab wounds to the **abdomen**, with their insides falling out. Galen had to put their **intestines** back in and sew them up.

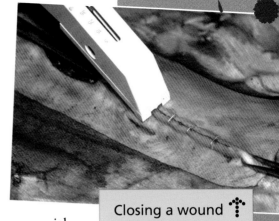

Closing a wound using staples.

Gladiators fought to entertain the Roman crowds ... and to keep surgeons like Galen busy.

catgut strong thread made from the intestines of sheep and used in surgery

The Middle Ages

This picture from 1465 shows an Arab doctor sealing a patient's sores with a hot iron.

The **Middle Ages** were a time of new ideas about medicine. These ideas came from Arab **surgeons** in the Middle East. Arab surgeons set bones and stitched wounds but they also did eye operations. They wrote down their new treatments. These surgery text books were taken to Europe where monks copied them. The books became important for training doctors.

By 1300, surgeons had learned a lot about the body. This was not just from books. Some doctors cut up dead bodies to see what went on inside them.

Ouch!

Nearly a thousand years ago, Arab surgeons pressed red-hot irons on to wounds. This was supposed to seal them up and stop them from going **septic**. They burnt off boils and skin **tumours** like this, too. These treatments often worked!

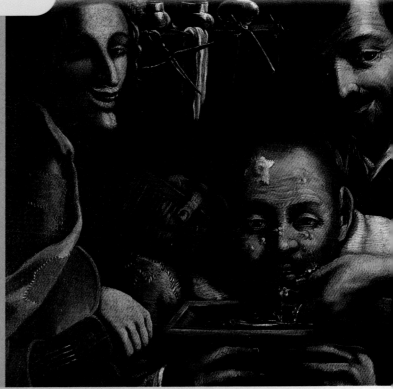

Word bank   **Middle Ages**   period of history roughly between AD 500 and AD 1500

A bad knight

An Arab doctor wrote this in 1150:

> I went to see a knight, who had a boil on his leg. I put a **dressing** on the leg and the boil began to heal. But then a European doctor came and said, "This doctor has no idea how to cure people."
>
> He sent for a strong man and an axe. The doctor put the knight's leg on a block of wood and told the strong man to cut the leg off cleanly. The blood and **marrow** spurted out and the knight died soon after.

Hit and miss

Arab surgeons were not keen to cut open patients. They knew how the shock and bleeding could kill. As a last resort they would carry out surgery after drugging the patient with **opium**. Opium is a drug made from poppies (below).

Surgeons cutting a boil on a man's head.

septic   getting infected with bacteria

tumour   abnormal growth or swelling in the body

On the move

From the 10th century, people who had trained themselves to be surgeons travelled around Europe. They made people pay to have broken bones set or teeth pulled out. They also did minor body surgery for a small fee.

Chop it off

Eight hundred years ago, there were many battles between Arabs and Europeans. **Surgeons** were kept busy treating the wounds of soldiers on the battlefields. They had to remove arrows stuck in soldiers' bodies. Pulling out arrow heads could rip **organs** and **blood vessels**.

Deadly infections would soon set in. The only way for surgeons to save lives was to chop off infected fingers, arms and legs. It was rare for patients to **survive**. Pain, shock and loss of blood could kill them quickly.

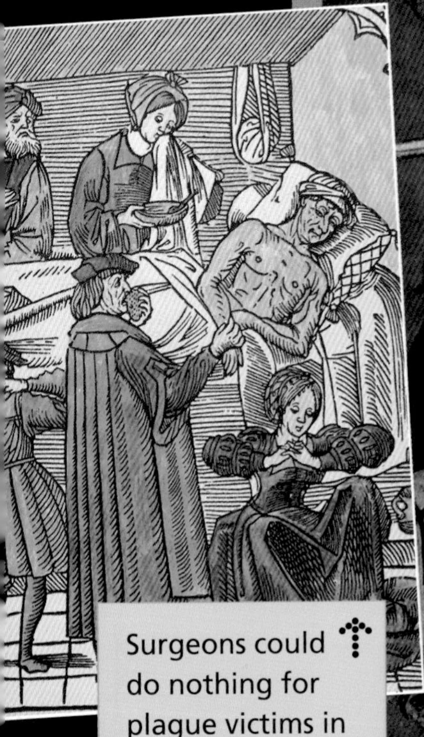

Surgeons could do nothing for plague victims in the Middle Ages.

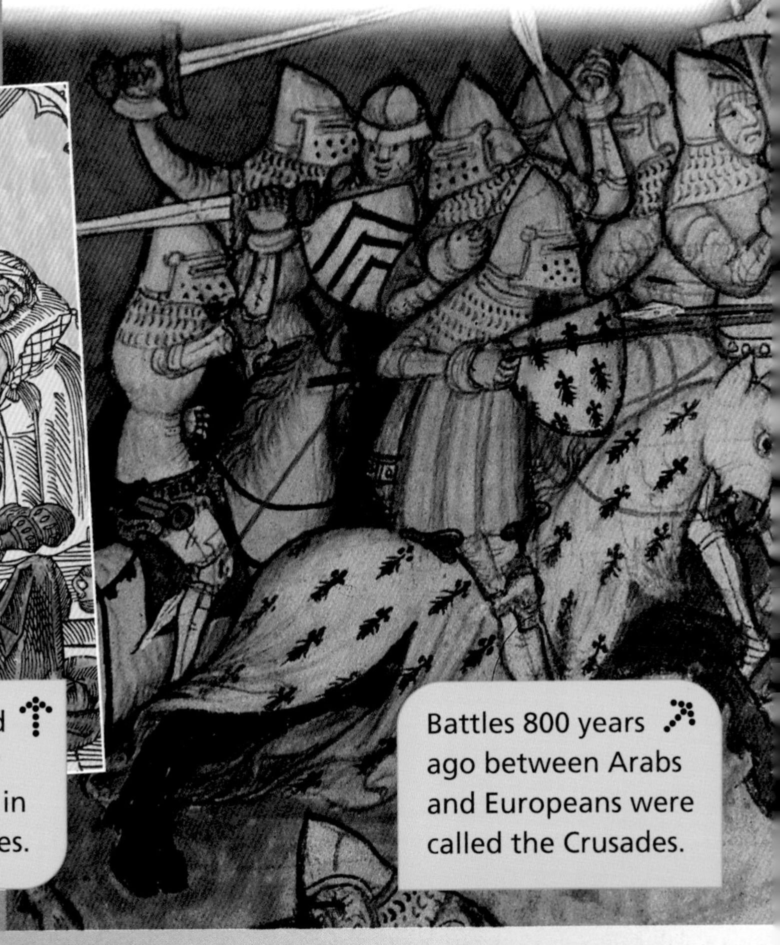

Battles 800 years ago between Arabs and Europeans were called the Crusades.

Word bank

abscess swollen infection full of pus

Sweet dreams

Some surgeons did try to make patients sleepy before they **amputated** a part of the body. But often mixtures of herbs, drugs and wine just meant the patient died more peacefully.

An English surgeon called John of Arderne made a mixture to send a patient to sleep. In 1376 he wrote:

> The man who is to be operated on should drink the whole bottle by a warm fire, where he will fall asleep. When you want him to wake, wash his face with salt and vinegar.

Saddle-sore

In the **Middle Ages** people travelled long distances on horses. Too long in the saddle could cause an **abscess** to grow on the **rectum**.

John of Arderne treated many infected rectums. He cut a hole between a patient's rectum and buttock to make emptying the **bowel** easier.

Riding a horse day after day gave many knights health problems.

blood vessels narrow tubes inside the body that carry blood
organ part inside the body that does a particular job

Gunshot wounds

The first hand guns were made in the 1300s. The problem for **surgeons** then was how to treat gunshot wounds. Digging out bullets caused wounds to get infected. The only cure was to cut off limbs to stop **gangrene** setting in.

To seal up gunshot wounds from bleeding or from getting gangrene, many doctors used boiling oil. They poured it into the wound. This may have stopped some bleeding but the painful burns often made wounds worse.

Sore with a saw

A surgeon in the 1500s wrote how to **amputate** the limbs of men with bad gunshot wounds.

After cutting through the skin and muscle you come to the bared bone. Cut it with a little saw. Then smooth the bone that the saw has made rough.

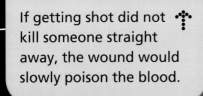

If getting shot did not kill someone straight away, the wound would slowly poison the blood.

Word bank

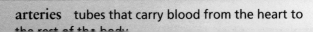

arteries   tubes that carry blood from the heart to

Burning oil

In the 1500s, the French surgeon Ambrose Paré realized hot oil caused too much damage.

I ran out of hot oil to put on the soldiers' wounds. Instead I put on a mixture of egg yolk, oil of roses and turpentine. What I found was beyond my wildest hope. They had little pain and their wounds were not inflamed. Yet those who had been given the hot oil were in dreadful pain. I decided never again to burn so cruelly the poor men who had been wounded.

Burning flesh

Ambrose Paré died in 1590. He wrote about how to stop the bleeding after cutting off an arm.

Tie up the veins and arteries quickly. I beg all surgeons not to use hot oil – and leave behind this old and cruel way of healing.

Gangrene can set in when an infection blocks off the blood supply to a part of the body.

gangrene   when flesh rots and dies due to infection or lack of blood supply

Blood, boils and

Did you know?

People thought that too much blood could make them ill. To keep healthy, they would need to bleed. Blood-letting was done by barbers. The usual way was to "breathe a vein" by tying a strap around the arm to make veins swell. The fattest vein was then opened with a blade and the blood spurted out.

From the 1500s to the 1700s you could get more than a hair cut from the local barber. He was called a **barber surgeon** and he used to cut out boils or make cuts in the skin. Bleeding was thought to do you good!

Barber surgeons had no real training. In 1540 the Company of Barber Surgeons was set up to try and change this. It was another 200 years before The Company of Surgeons was set up in London for true **surgeons**. In 1800 this became the Royal College of Surgeons.

In 1556 Bruegel painted this picture to make fun of barber surgeons.

Word bank **barber surgeon** barber who also did minor surgery,

Barber surgery

After the barber surgeon finished an operation, the bloody bandages were hung out to dry. They were pegged to a post outside the shop. The wind would twirl the bandages into a red and white spiral pattern. This pattern was later used on painted poles to show where a barber worked.

Some barbers would even display a basin of blood outside their shop. This was to show they did **blood-letting**.

Some barbers' shops today still display red and white poles, just like the blood and bandages of the barber surgeons.

Samuel Pepys wrote a lot about life in London in the 1600s.

Being bled

We know a lot about life in London in the 1600s from a diary written by Samuel Pepys. He was bled by a barber.

4 May 1662

Mr Holliard came to let me bleed. I began to be sick, but lying on my back, I was soon well again. I gave him 5 shillings and he left.

blood-letting   cutting the skin or a vein to let blood flow out

All in a day's work

There was plenty of blood around in 17th-century London. There were only two main hospitals but they did not have operating theatres as we know them today. Most surgery was done in people's homes or in barber shops. Proper painkillers and **anaesthetic** were still unheard of.

Joseph Binns was a **surgeon** from 1633 to 1663. He often wrote notes about his patients. One of his notebooks lists some of his patients' problems:

77 patients with swellings
15 with battle wounds
14 injured at work
41 hurt in fights
19 fallen from horses

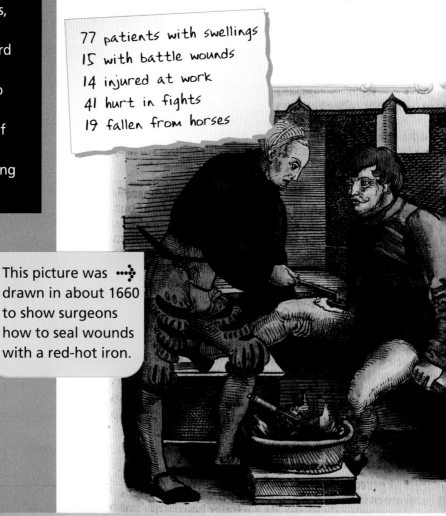

This picture was ⋯⟡ drawn in about 1660 to show surgeons how to seal wounds with a red-hot iron.

Word bank   anaesthetic   drugs to make patients sleep or to make
treatment less painful

Red-hot poker

Most of Binns' patients were treated in his own house. Many stayed for a month or longer. **Lancing** a boil would be a painful treatment. Binns would dig his **scalpel** into the swelling and drain out the **pus**. Or he might poke it with a red-hot poker. Although the heat may have helped to **sterilize** the wound, the pain would have been terrible.

Binns also did "wet cupping" on patients. This involved pushing heated metal cups on to the cut skin of a patient's back. Blood collected in the cups. This was thought to remove bad fluid from the body.

Burning flesh

Even today doctors sometimes burn a patient. This is called **cauterizing**. It is only used in minor cases, like closing off a bleeding vein in the nose or to burn off a wart. This is done with a chemical, a heated electric wire or with **laser** surgery.

Surgeons still use cauterizing to burn away some skin problems.

sterilize   make clean by killing germs

ulcer   open sore, often full of pus

The kidneys

The two kidneys are found in the lower back on either side of the spine. They filter out waste from the body and keep the blood clean. If stones grow in a kidney, they can cause a blockage. This needs treatment to stop the kidney swelling and getting damaged.

Under the knife

A lump that grows in the kidney is called a kidney stone. It is painful if it starts to move. Today this is easy to deal with but for Samuel Pepys it was a matter of life and death. In 1658 he needed an operation to remove a kidney stone.

There were no painkillers but he drank rose water with egg-white and **liquorice**. This was thought to be good for the kidneys. Samuel **survived** the surgery and kept his kidney stone on display. Every year he held a party to celebrate his survival.

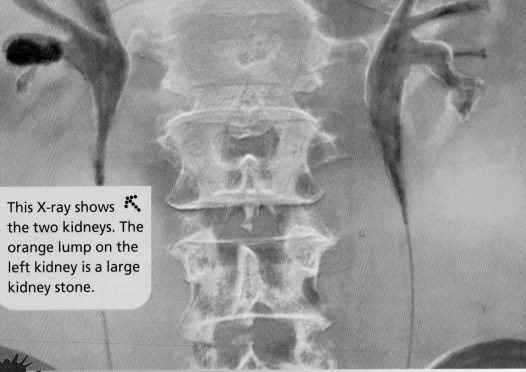

This X-ray shows the two kidneys. The orange lump on the left kidney is a large kidney stone.

Word bank

calcium crystal very small part of the material that

Kidneys on the table

In 1663 Samuel Pepys went to watch a **surgeon** cutting open a dead body. He wanted to see what kidneys looked like and where kidney stones grew. He wrote about the dead body in his diary.

It was a strong fellow, who had been hanged for robbery. I touched the dead body with my bare hand. It felt cold and unpleasant. Then the kidneys were placed on the table. There, the surgeon showed me the kidney stone and the cutting he did to remove it.

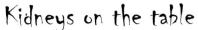

Kidney stones are not always smooth and round.

It is only in recent times that patients have had a good chance of **surviving** surgery. A lot of the knowledge we have is because of key people and events throughout history.

Body snatching

The training of **surgeons** improved in the 1700s. Medical students cut open dead bodies to see how they worked. The problem was how to get hold of fresh dead bodies to use. Some students got their own – by digging them up from graves! Surgeons paid good money for a dead body to use with their students.

Butcher

Burke and Hare were killers. Children sang:

"Burke is the butcher, Hare is the thief, Knox is the doctor who buys the beef."

But it was not beef they dealt in – it was human bodies!

Doctor Knox bought ⋯ many bodies to use in his talks to student doctors.

Word bank   **pauper**   poor person

Ask no questions

Robert Knox was a surgeon in Edinburgh, Scotland in the 1820s. Students paid to go to his talks where he cut open bodies to show all the **organs**.

Two thieves called Burke and Hare realized they could make easy money. They dug up graves and sold the bodies to Knox. Before long, they started to strangle their own victims, put them in sacks and sell them to Knox.

Burke and Hare killed at least fourteen people, while Knox asked no questions. When the police called, Knox told them how he got the bodies. They let him off and arrested Burke and Hare.

Fresh supplies

Burke and Hare were not the only body snatchers. In 1831, Bishop and Williams were hanged. They had supplied London medical schools with between 500 and 1000 bodies.

The Anatomy Act in 1832 stopped grave robbing in the UK. Bodies of dead prisoners or **paupers** could now be used to train surgeons (below).

Selling dead bodies to surgeons was once a way to make quick money.

25

Dull the pain

Pain and **trauma** killed many patients on the operating table. Major surgery was just not possible. A few drugs like **opium** or alcohol helped to dull some of the pain. But **surgeons** had to work fast to reduce the agony of cutting, sawing and sewing.

Horace Wells was a dentist in Connecticut, USA. In 1845 he used a gas called **nitrous oxide** to make a patient sleep. The following year, another US dentist used **ether** for the same purpose. It was the start of pain-free surgery.

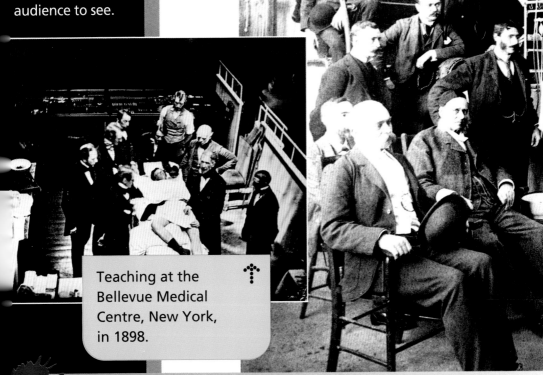

Teaching at the Bellevue Medical Centre, New York, in 1898.

Word bank

ether   chemical first used as an anaesthetic in the 1800s

Painless surgery

Putting patients to sleep was a big risk. Too much ether could kill them. Too little would mean they would wake up in the middle of the operation.

Ether began to be used for major surgery. In 1846, in the USA, 21-year-old Alice Mohan was put to sleep with ether. Dr George Hayward had to cut off her leg above the knee. When she woke, he showed her the sawn-off leg to prove the operation was safely over. This was the start of effective **anaesthetic**.

A new drug

A real breakthrough in surgery came in 1847. James Simpson, a Scottish doctor, discovered that **chloroform** made a good anaesthetic. Ten years later Queen Victoria was given chloroform during the birth of her eighth child.

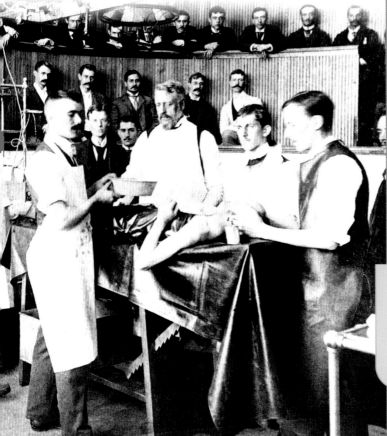

A patient under anaesthetic awaits surgery at the Metropolitan Hospital in London.

nitrous oxide   colourless gas used as an anaesthetic

Cut it out

While **surgeons** in the USA were trying out **anaesthetic** in the 1840s, one London surgeon carried on without it for a while.

Robert Liston was well known for being the fastest surgeon around. He would tell his students at the start of the operation, "Time me." They set their watches and away he went. While he used a saw to cut off a leg, he would often hold the **scalpel** between his teeth. Once he cut out a patient's huge 20 kilogram **tumour** in just 4 minutes. People who came to watch him often fainted.

Robert Liston cut off arms and legs in record time.

All fingers and thumbs

Robert Liston once **amputated** a leg in less than 2 minutes. But that was not all. In his rush he also cut off the fingers of his young assistant who was holding the patient! Anaesthetic soon made his work far easier because he could take more time.

Operating theatres were not very **high-tech** places in the early 1900s.

Word bank

appendix organ attached to the large intestine; it has no use in the human body

Progress

During the 1800s, surgeons began to perform new operations.

- During the 1870s, an Austrian called Theodor Billroth was the first surgeon to remove throat tumours. In 1881, he removed part of a cancer patient's stomach. It was a success. By 1890, his team had done 41 operations like this with a 46 per cent **survival** rate.
- In 1882, Carl Langenbach of Berlin, Germany, removed the **gall bladder** of a 42-year-old man with gallstones.
- In 1883 the first **appendix** was removed with success. Abraham Groves did this operation in Canada. The patient was a twelve-year-old boy.

Appendix

If the appendix gets infected, it can cause pain. This was once very dangerous. As a result of progress made in surgery by doctors such as Abraham Groves, the appendix could be removed safely. By 1924, Groves had done 6000 appendix operations.

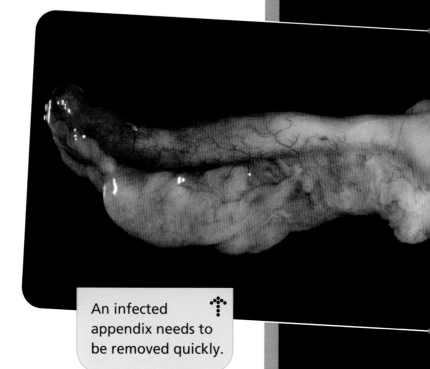

An infected appendix needs to be removed quickly.

gall bladder   organ that stores bile, which helps in digestion
high-tech   using the very latest technology

Keep it clean

It was a long time before **surgeons** knew about germs. After surgery, patients often fell ill from infected wounds. Surgeons did not realize poor **hygiene** was killing their patients. They went from one patient to another without washing, passing on deadly **bacteria**.

By 1860, the English surgeon Thomas Spencer Wells insisted on washing before each operation. He would not let anyone into the operating room if they had been near a dead body in the last week. He saw how patients got much better if everything was kept clean.

Surgeons today have to "scrub up" carefully before every operation.

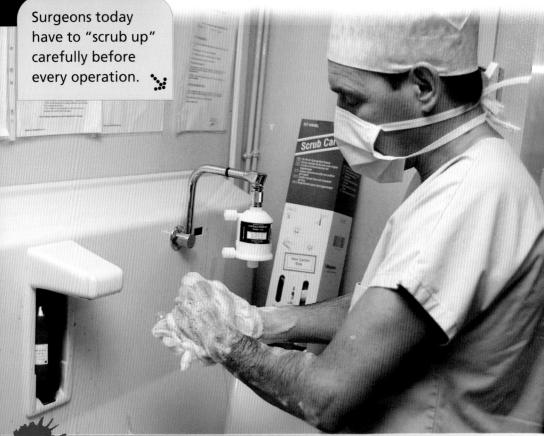

Word bank

antiseptic   substance that stops harmful bacteria growing and spreading disease

Killing germs

In 1865, when James Greenless was eleven years old, a cart ran over him in Glasgow, Scotland and broke his leg. Wounds like this usually became so badly infected that the whole leg had to be cut off. Instead, surgeon Joseph Lister put a special **dressing** on the leg. This contained a **disinfectant** called carbolic acid. The wound did not go **septic** and James recovered.

Lister wrote about the results of this operation. Soon other surgeons read about his **antiseptic**. He also showed how important it was to disinfect tools and stitches. He sprayed the whole operating theatre with carbolic spray.

Recovery

More of Lister's patients began to survive surgery when he used antiseptics.

Years	Total cases	Recovered	Died
1864 to 1866	35	19	16
1867 to 1870	40	34	6

Joseph Lister used carbolic spray to make surgery antiseptic.

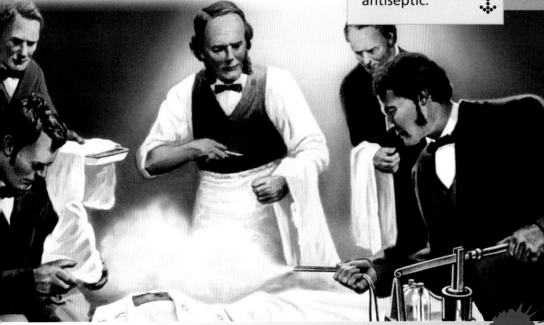

disinfectant   chemical that destroys germs

New ideas

For hundreds of years, doctors and **surgeons** thought diseases spread in "bad air". They did not know that tiny living germs or **bacteria** bred in warm, wet and dirty places. Open wounds were ideal breeding places.

A French scientist called Louis Pasteur tried to find out how germs bred. He discovered that tiny bacteria made wounds turn **septic**. His work was very important in showing surgeons how they needed to work in **sterile** places. In 1874, Pasteur showed that surgical tools could be **sterilized** in boiling water or by passing them through a flame.

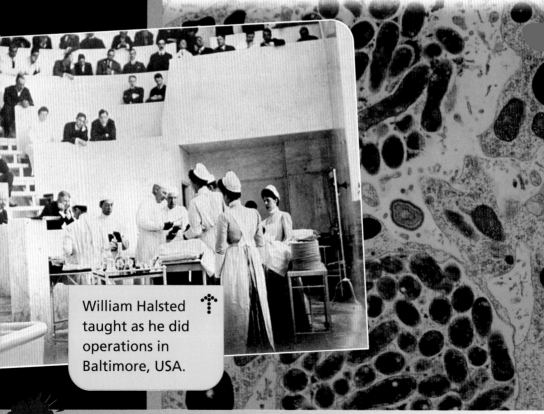

William Halsted taught as he did operations in Baltimore, USA.

aseptic   sterilized air, clothes and tools in a surgeon's operating room

Germ-free

A German scientist proved Louis Pasteur's ideas right. Robert Koch grew all kinds of germs and studied them under a microscope. He found out which bacteria made wounds turn septic.

Koch found that hot steam killed more germs than carbolic acid. This led to **aseptic** surgery. It became very important to have strict rules about how to keep the operating room clean. Bandages, tools and clothes were all sterilized to remove dirt and germs. With the risk of infection now falling, operations got bigger and bolder. These new ideas led to great progress.

Modern masks stop surgeons breathing out bacteria into open wounds.

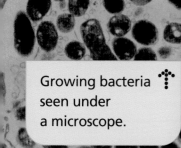
Growing bacteria seen under a microscope.

Dressed to kill germs

We now know that a surgeon coughing and sneezing over a patient's open wound can cause infection. Modern masks are treated with chemicals to kill the germs the surgeon breathes out. Even coughs and sneezes cannot harm the patient.

The story of the Battle of Gettysburg was told in the film *Gettysburg* in 1993.

Some of the most terrible wounds that **surgeons** have to treat happen during wars. War injuries have meant surgery has had to improve.

Field hospitals were set up in tents close to battles. Bullet wounds soon became infected so surgeons had to deal with patients as fast as they could. If **amputation** was not done in the first 24 hours after an injury, a soldier was likely to die. Even then there was only a 50 per cent chance of survival. Surgeons had to keep finding ways of increasing their speed.

Bloody battles

The American **Civil War** started in 1861. The North and the South had different views about keeping slaves and the best way to run the country. Four years later the 23 Union states in the North beat the 11 Confederate states in the South. Six hundred thousand men were killed during this civil war.

Surgeons 150 years ago in the American Civil War had to learn fast.

Word bank

civil war when soldiers from the same country fight against each other

In the field

In May 1864 a soldier wrote in his diary about a field hospital.

I saw one man with an arm off at the shoulder, with maggots crawling in the flesh. Surgeons wore **linen** covered with blood from top to bottom.

Arms and legs were flung out on to a pile of **severed limbs**. It was more than six feet wide and three feet high.

With his arm or leg sawn off, each man was passed to the next table, where other surgeons finished the bandaging. Heaven forbid that I should ever again witness such a sight.

Gettysburg

During the American Civil War over 7000 men were killed in the Battle of Gettysburg. Carl Schurz watched a surgeon at work after the battle.

The surgeon snatched his knife from between his teeth and wiped it across his blood-stained apron. After cutting off an arm, he looked around with a sigh and said, "next!"

linen   type of cloth, often made into white sheets
severed limbs   arms and legs that have been cut off

35

World War 1

World War 1 (from 1914 to 1918) saw some of the worst injuries of any war. The bombing of soldiers stuck in muddy **trenches** kept **surgeons** working day and night.

Field hospitals were in filthy places so wounds quickly became infected. **Gangrene** was a real problem and surgeons often had to cut off soldiers' arms and legs. At least there was now more reliable **anaesthetic**. Even so, surgeons thought they were doing well if only half of their patients **survived**. Surgeons had to cut off more limbs in World War 1 than in any war before.

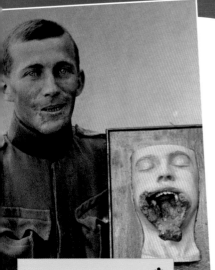

A German soldier stands next to a wax model showing his injuries before surgery.

Fast developments

As a result of war, surgery improved. Surgeons got better at giving **blood transfusions**, which saved many lives. About 10 per cent of wounds in World War 1 were head wounds. Because of this, eye, face, ear, nose and throat surgery had to develop quickly.

Word bank

antibiotic   substance made from bacteria that kills other harmful bacteria

Breakthrough

For the first time in field hospitals, surgeons used new developments in science to help them. **Portable** X-ray machines let them see bullets stuck inside patients. This really improved success in removing the bullets. But the wounds still had to be stopped from going **septic**.

One scientist began to think about this problem. He saw many soldiers' infected wounds and realized that some germs seemed to kill other germs. His name was Alexander Fleming. He went on to discover **antibiotics** – one of the greatest medical discoveries of all time.

X-rays

Being able to see inside a body without cutting it open was a great advance. In 1912, X-rays allowed a New York surgeon to remove a nail from a boy's lungs. A few years later the scientist Marie Curie fitted army cars with X-ray machines.

Soldiers in the trenches in World War 1 were sitting targets for bombs and gunfire.

The earliest X-ray machines were used in World War 1.

portable   easily moved or carried
trenches   ditches dug by soldiers as shelter from enemy attack

In World War 2, burns covering half the body were nearly always **fatal**. New ways of treating burn victims had to develop quickly. Many pilots escaped from burning planes but needed years of surgery to their hands and faces.

World War 2

Surgeons had always thought that operating on the heart was too dangerous. But things changed during World War 2 (from 1939 to 1945). Army doctors had to deal with **shrapnel** wounds to all parts of the body, including the heart. Now they had **antibiotics**, good **anaesthetics** and **blood transfusions**. Some tried operating on the heart for the first time.

Dwight Harken was a US Army surgeon. He tried to find a way to cut into a beating heart so he could dig out the shrapnel with his finger. At first he practised on animals. Then he operated on soldiers. Most of them survived.

People stuck in bombed buildings were badly burned.

Word bank   **fatal**   resulting in death

Firebomb

In World War 2 firebombs burned many people. Pilots who survived crashes would often be so badly burned there seemed to be no hope. But Archibald McIndoe was a surgeon who tried out new ways of treating airmen with bad burns. He changed the lives of more than 600 men who never thought they would **survive**.

McIndoe performed many new types of skin surgery. That often meant at least 25 operations on each patient. Slowly their wounds and scars healed. McIndoe's patients formed a special club, called the Guinea Pig Club. Some members still meet today!

New skin

McIndoe cut healthy skin from one part of a patient's body and planted it over a burn. But sometimes the new skin died from lack of blood supply.

So McIndoe simply kept the new piece of skin attached to another part of the body to keep it alive (left). In time the new skin began to grow on its own.

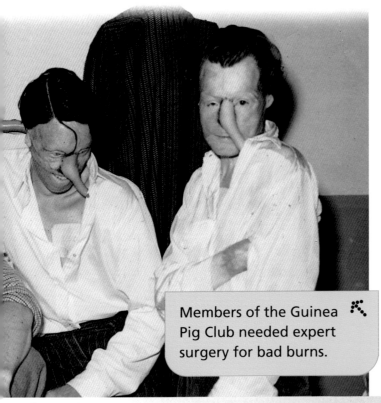

Members of the Guinea Pig Club needed expert surgery for bad burns.

shrapnel fragments of metal thrown out in an explosion

Modern times

There has been more progress in surgery in the last 50 years than at any other time in history.

Transplants

Christiaan Barnard studied heart surgery in the USA. He went to South Africa to set up a heart unit. In 1967 he took the heart from a dead road-accident victim and put it into a 55-year-old man. This was the first operation of its kind.

Sadly the patient died eighteen days later from **pneumonia**. He had been given drugs to help stop his body rejecting the new heart. But these had weakened his ability to fight infection.

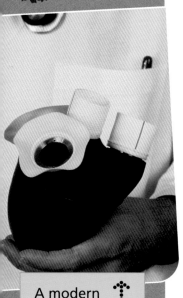

A modern artificial heart.

New parts

People used to think that fitting a dead person's heart into another person was just impossible. Replacing worn-out parts with new ones was treating the human body like a car! But now transplants happen every day. Even **artificial** hearts are used.

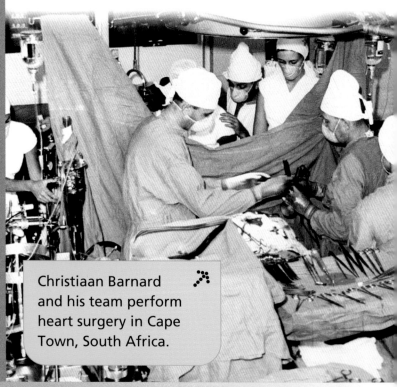

Christiaan Barnard and his team perform heart surgery in Cape Town, South Africa.

Word bank

pancreas   organ near the stomach that controls sugar in the blood

New hearts

Christiaan Barnard did not give up. One of his next patients lived for over eighteen months after similar surgery. Even so, many patients' bodies rejected their new hearts so transplants stopped.

In 1974 a scientist in Norway found a new drug to stop the body rejecting new **organs**. Heart transplants became more successful. Since the late 1980s, most patients have **survived** for more than two years after this kind of surgery.

Christiaan Barnard proved that heart transplants could work. Today heart-lung machines make heart surgery much safer. They take over the body's blood-pumping and breathing to give the **surgeons** more time to operate.

Record-breaker

Danny Canal's **intestines** stopped working when he was eight years old. Then his other organs failed. In 1998, aged thirteen, he was given a new stomach, **liver**, **pancreas**, and intestine in Miami, USA. But these failed, too. He needed the four-organ transplant three times in seven weeks. He now leads a normal life.

Organs from a dead victim of a road accident are rushed to a hospital to be used for a transplant.

HUMAN ORGANS

pneumonia   disease of the lungs that makes it difficult to breathe

Keyhole surgery

It used to take weeks for wounds to heal after surgery, leaving big scars and scabs. A lot of modern surgery now leaves hardly a mark. Keyhole surgery is an operation through a very small cut, maybe only a few centimetres long.

Surgeons today can see what is going on inside a body using a tiny camera. This is put on the end of a fine tube called an **endoscope**. The image is shown on a TV screen. The surgeon watches the screen while doing the operation.

DARKNESS STAR TO HAVE KEYHOLE SURGERY

Justin Hawkins, lead singer of The Darkness, is to have surgery on his throat.

The singer had to cancel two shows on the band's US tour due to a throat problem. Surgeons will insert a tiny tube into his throat. They expect him to make a full recovery.

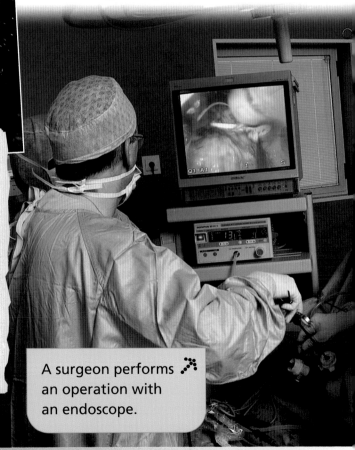

A surgeon performs an operation with an endoscope.

Word bank   **cornea** clear outer layer at the front of the eyeball

Laser technology

Even the finest **scalpel** in the best surgeon's hand can slip. But a **laser** beam can cut much more accurately. This has made eye surgery today much safer. In fact, some people no longer need to wear glasses after a quick zap from a laser.

One of the newest types of eye laser cuts through the front of the eyeball, called the **cornea**. A thin layer is sliced off to leave a flap. This lets the laser target the tissue underneath. The flap is then put back and it grows again. The patient can see again almost straight away.

Fast work

Kidney stones can now be removed through a very fine tube. The tube is passed into the kidney and takes out small stones easily. Larger stones need to be broken up first using **ultra-sound**. The operation can take as little as fifteen minutes.

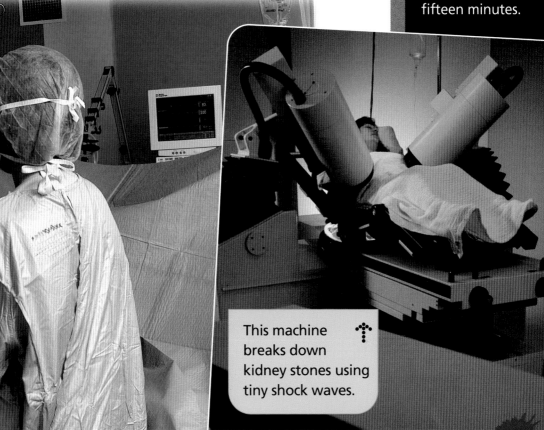

This machine breaks down kidney stones using tiny shock waves.

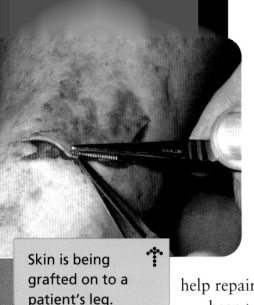

Skin is being grafted on to a patient's leg.

Plastic surgery

Plastic surgery is an operation which helps to rebuild part of someone's body. Skin damage from burns, disease or injury can now usually be repaired. **High-tech** tools are used to join up nerves and repair the skin.

Plastic surgery can also be used to help repair hands and fingers after they have been torn off in accidents. Parts of the body can now be rebuilt after **tumours** have been cut out. This is called **reconstructive** surgery. It is a growing part of today's medicine.

Metal prongs help to straighten a diseased finger.

Saving skin

The first plastic surgeons tried to repair wounds by using skin-flaps to reshape damaged skin.

Skin **grafting** still happens today. It takes healthy skin from one part of the body and plants it somewhere else. But it still takes time for healthy tissue to grow and for scars to heal.

Word bank   **graft**   piece of living tissue that is transplanted with surgery

Saving a face

In 1997 a farmer caught her hair in a milking machine in Victoria, Australia. It ripped off her face and **scalp**. Only her chin and one ear were left in one piece. Her face and scalp were packed in ice and rushed with her to hospital. Wayne Morrison, a top plastic surgeon, began to reattach the woman's face.

The operation took 25 hours and the patient needed 9 litres of blood. This was one of the first operations of its kind. The **surgeon** said it might even be possible to transplant faces one day.

Changing faces

Some people have plastic surgery to make them look like film stars. In 2004, a TV programme was shown in the USA called *I want a famous face*. Two brothers had surgery on their faces to make them look like Brad Pitt. They needed new noses, cheek **implants** and a lot of money!

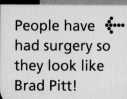

People have had surgery so they look like Brad Pitt!

scalp   skin covering the top of the head, where hair grows

Unblocking tubes

Plumbers spend a lot of time unblocking pipes. Many **surgeons** have to do the same. Our bodies are full of narrow tubes. If they clog up, they cannot work and our bodies are at risk.

If **blood vessels** get clogged with fatty lumps, the heart is put under strain. An operation called an **angioplasty** may be needed. This involves a fine tube with a tiny balloon on the end. It is pushed along a blood vessel until it reaches the blockage. The balloon is then **inflated** to push open the blood vessel.

An inside job

Tiny tools on the end of fine wire can now be pushed along blood vessels inside the body. They can then snip or burn away anything that should not be there. This can be done with the patient awake and without leaving so much as a tiny scar.

A tiny balloon is pumped up in an angioplasty.

Word bank

angioplasty   surgical unblocking of a blood vessel
colon   lower part of the large intestine

Fire down below!

Surgery used to be necessary for people with pains in the **colon** or **bowel**. Now it is a matter of pushing a tube up through the **rectum**. This is called a **colonoscopy** and uses an **endoscope**. The surgeon can then look for signs of cancer in the colon, for **ulcers** or any bleeding.

To let the endoscope move through the tubes, air is pumped into the rectum. Then a burning tool can get rid of problems. A few years ago this sometimes set fire to the **methane gas** in the colon. Now patients have the methane gas removed from the colon before the colonoscopy.

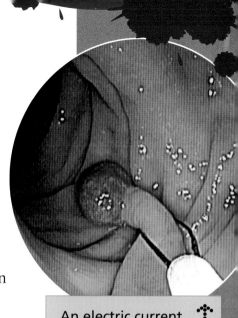

An electric current passes through a fine wire to cut off and seal up harmful lumps inside the body.

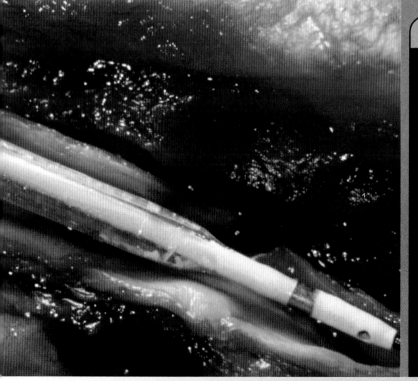

Surgical sparks

In 1995, 76-year-old Frank Axford woke up from an operation for colon cancer. He was shocked to find burns on his bottom. A tool had set fire to surgical spirit on the operating table. Frank said, "My backside must have gone up like a Christmas pudding!"

colonoscopy   looking inside the colon with an endoscope
methane gas   gas that is sometimes released in the gut

47

Zipping up

Stitches and scars have always been part of surgery. It would be useful if our bodies had a zip that could be zipped up after an operation!

Today surgeons can use a new surgical zipper to seal up wounds. The special zip is stuck on to the skin and simply zipped up.

Latest news

Surgery is always in the news. New operations are being done all the time. These raise questions such as: Can this really work? Is it right to do this?

SURGEONS PLAN NEW LIVER TRANSPLANTS

The problem with transplants is the lack of **donors**. Someone has to die before an **organ** can be used. But UK **surgeons** can now use part of a living donor's liver. Donors give half of their own liver, which regrows in a few weeks. Many relatives are keen to donate part of their own organs to help a loved one.

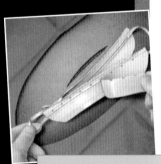

The Medizip is a special zipper that seals up surgical wounds.

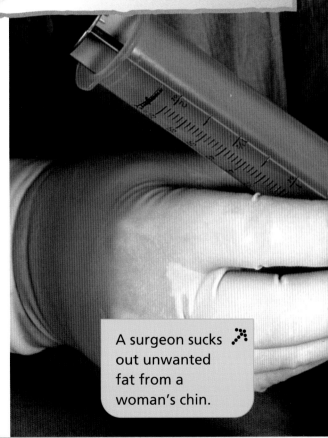

A surgeon sucks out unwanted fat from a woman's chin.

Word bank

donor person whose body parts or blood are used in transplant operations

Surgical slimming

Surgery used to be the last resort to save lives. Now it is even used to help people look slimmer. But such surgery has risks. A healthy diet and exercise are far safer.

Some **obese** patients have lost fat by having it sucked out. This is called **liposuction**. The surgeon inserts a tool under the skin to suck out the fatty fluid. Other patients have their stomach stapled to make it smaller. Then they can only eat small amounts of food. This is not the best way to lose weight.

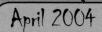

April 2004

LIVING BANDAGES TO TREAT BURN VICTIMS

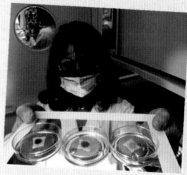

People with severe burns could now be healed with living bandages made of their own skin cells.

UK scientists are behind the new treatment, called Myskin. It uses healthy skin cells grown on small discs. These are then planted on the wound, helping new skin to grow.

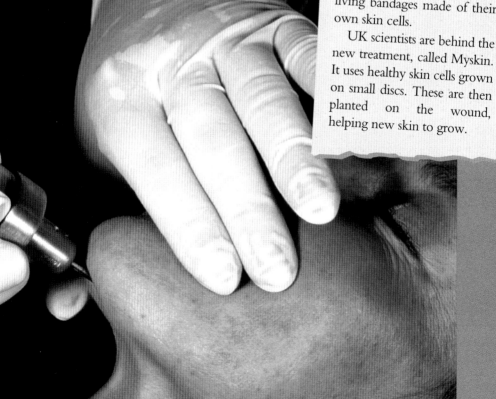

liposuction removing fat from under the skin by sucking it out through a tube

49

In 1999, US **surgeons** performed the first hand transplant. They attached a dead person's hand to a 37-year-old man. The patient lost his own hand four years earlier in an accident. It took fifteen hours to attach the bones with metal plates. Surgeons had to connect the nerves and **arteries** with small stitches.

And finally...

In an emergency, surgery may be the only answer, even if there are no **antiseptics** and **anaesthetic** nearby.

Self-surgery

In 2003, Aron Ralston went mountain hiking alone in Utah, USA. Miles from anywhere, a boulder fell and trapped his arm. It pinned him down and there was no way he could get free. He would have to lie there and starve to death. He decided to use a blunt penknife for surgery that took days. He slowly cut off his own arm, right through the bone. He escaped, got medical help and lived!

Aron Ralston in Colorado, USA, recovering from his home-made surgery.

Surgery in the air

In 1995, Paula Dixon was on a flight from Hong Kong to London. She felt so ill that a call went out to see if there were any doctors on the plane. Dr Angus Wallace and Dr Tom Wong rushed to the rescue.

Paula's lung had stopped working and needed quick treatment. The doctors got a wire coat hanger and dipped the end in brandy to **sterilize** it. Then they poked it into her chest. They drained her lung through a tube into a water bottle. Paula made a full recovery.

The future

If the last 50 years have brought such huge changes to surgery – what will the next 50 years bring? Perhaps there will be body banks of spare parts. Like cars, we will just get fitted with a new part whenever we need it. Who knows what tomorrow will bring?

Surgeons look to the future...

51

Find out more

Did you know?

- In 1998 a man had a 20-centimetre knife removed from his skull and lived! It was the largest object ever to be removed from a human skull.

- The largest **gall bladder** ever removed weighed 10.4 kilograms.

- The largest **tumour** removed intact weighed an amazing 137.6 kilograms!

Books

Groundbreakers: Alexander Fleming,
  Steve Parker (Heinemann Library, 2001)
Hidden Life: What's Living Inside Your Body?,
  Andrew Solway (Heinemann Library, 2004)
Microlife: Scientists and Discoveries,
  Robert Sneddon (Heinemann Library, 2000)

Using the Internet

Explore the Internet to find out more about medicine through the ages. You can use a search engine, such as www.yahooligans.com, and type in keywords such as:

- gladiator
- barber surgeon
- antiseptic

Search tips

There are billions of pages on the Internet so it can be difficult to find exactly what you are looking for.

These search tips will help you find useful websites more quickly:

- Know exactly what you want to find out about first.
- Use two to six keywords in a search, putting the most important words first.
- Be precise. Only use names of people, places or things.

Glossary

abdomen area of the body below the chest, containing the stomach

Aborigine native Australian person

abscess swollen infection full of pus

amputate cut off

anaesthetic drugs to make patients sleep or to make treatment less painful

angioplasty surgical unblocking of a blood vessel

antibiotic substance made from bacteria that kills other harmful bacteria

antiseptic substance that stops harmful bacteria growing and spreading disease

appendix organ attached to the large intestine; it has no use in the human body

arteries tubes that carry blood from the heart to the rest of the body

artificial man-made

aseptic sterilized air, clothes and tools in a surgeon's operating room

bacteria group of tiny living things, some can cause disease

barber surgeon barber who also did minor surgery, mainly for the poor

blood-letting cutting the skin or a vein to let blood flow out

blood transfusion taking some blood from one person and putting it into another

blood vessels narrow tubes inside the body that carry blood

bowel part of the intestine where body waste is held before being let out of the body

Caesarean born by being cut from the mother's womb

calcium crystal very small part of the material that makes up bones and teeth

catgut strong thread made from the intestines of sheep and used in surgery

cauterize burn a wound with a heated instrument

chloroform colourless liquid with a strong smell, used as an anaesthetic

civil war when soldiers from the same country fight against each other

colon lower part of the large intestine

colonoscopy looking inside the colon with an endoscope

coma like being in a very deep sleep, usually due to injury or disease

cornea clear outer layer at the front of the eyeball

disinfectant chemical that destroys germs

donor person whose body parts or blood are used in transplant operations

dressing soft bandage put on to a sore or wound

endoscope instrument for viewing inside a body

ether chemical first used as an anaesthetic in the 1800s

fatal resulting in death

field hospital make-shift hospital, often in a tent near the battlefield

forceps surgical pincers used to hold and grasp things

gall bladder organ that stores bile, which helps in digestion

gangrene when flesh rots and dies due to infection or lack of blood supply

gladiator Roman trained to fight with weapons

graft piece of living tissue that is transplanted with surgery

high-tech using the very latest technology

hygiene standards of cleanliness

implant material put under the skin to change the body shape

inflamed infected, red and sore

inflate fill up with air

intestines part of the body that goes from the stomach to the bowel, where food is digested

lancing piercing with a sharp point

laser very strong beam of light, used in surgery for burning or cutting

linen type of cloth, often made into white sheets

liposuction removing fat from under the skin by sucking it out through a tube

liquorice plant root that is used in many medicines and in cooking

liver organ in the body involved in the digestion process

marrow soft fatty jelly inside bones

methane gas gas that is sometimes released in the gut

Middle Ages period of history roughly between AD 500 and AD 1500

nitrous oxide colourless gas used as an anaesthetic

obese very overweight

opium drug made from opium poppies, used to help people relax and to relieve pain

organ part inside the body that does a particular job

pancreas organ near the stomach that controls sugar in the blood

pauper poor person

pneumonia disease of the lungs that makes it difficult to breathe

portable easily moved or carried

pressure force that builds up in a space and cannot escape

pus thick yellow or greenish foul-smelling liquid made by infected wounds

reconstructive putting something back together again

rectum end part of the large intestine, connected to the anus

scalp skin covering the top of the head, where hair grows

scalpel knife with a small sharp blade

septic getting infected with bacteria

severed limbs arms and legs that have been cut off

shrapnel fragments of metal thrown out in an explosion

sterile free from germs

sterilize make clean by killing germs

surgeon doctor who operates on the body and treats injuries

survive stay alive despite danger and difficulties

trauma severe shock and distress

trenches ditches dug by soldiers as shelter from enemy attack

trepanning drilling a hole through the skull

tumour abnormal growth or swelling in the body

ulcer open sore, often full of pus

ultra-sound very high sound waves that we cannot hear

womb part of the female body where a baby grows

Index

abscesses, boils and
  ulcers 12, 13, 14, 15,
  18, 20, 21
American Civil War
  34–35
amputation 10, 13, 14,
  15, 16, 28, 34, 35, 36
anaesthetics 20, 27,
  28, 36, 38
ancient times 6–11
angioplasty 46
antibiotics 36, 37, 38
antiseptics 30, 31
appendix 29
Arab surgeons 12,
  13, 14
aseptic surgery 32, 33

bacteria 30, 32, 33
barber surgeons 18–19
Barnard, Christiaan
  40–41
battle injuries 14,
  34–37, 38, 39
blood transfusions
  36, 38
blood-letting 18, 19
body snatchers 24–25
bullet wounds 16,
  34, 37
burn victims 38, 39,
  44, 49
burning wounds 12,
  16, 17, 20, 21

Caesarean birth 10
chloroform 27
colonoscopy 47

emergency situations
  50–51
endoscope 42, 47
ether 26, 27
eye surgery 43

Fleming, Alexander 37

Galen 11
gangrene 16, 17, 36
gowns and masks
  32, 33
Greeks and Romans
  10–11

heart surgery 38, 40

infection 12, 13, 14,
  16, 30, 31, 32, 33,
  34, 36, 37

keyhole surgery 42
kidney stones 22,
  23, 43

laser surgery 21, 43
liposuction 49
Lister, Joseph 30, 31

Medizip 48
Middle Ages 12–17

operating theatres 26,
  28, 30, 31
opium 13, 26

Pasteur, Louis 32
Pepys, Samuel 19,
  22–23
plaster casts 9
plastic surgery 39,
  44–45

reconstructive surgery
  44

scalpels 4, 8, 21, 28,
  43
self-surgery 50
skin grafting 39,
  44, 49
sterilization 21, 32, 33
stitches and staples
  8, 10, 11, 48

training 18, 24, 25, 26
transplants 40, 41, 45,
  48, 50
trepanning 6–7
tumours 12, 13, 26,
  28, 29, 44, 52

ultra-sound 23, 43

World Wars 36–39

X-rays 22, 37